Imagine a World

Sheila Nielsen

BookLeaf Publishing

India | USA | UK

Imagine a World © 2023 Sheila Nielsen

All rights reserved.

No part of this publication may be reproduced, stored in a retrieval system, or transmitted, in any form or by any means, electronic, mechanical, photocopying, recording or otherwise, without the prior written permission of the presenters.

Sheila Nielsen asserts the moral right to be identified as author of this work.

Presentation by *BookLeaf Publishing*

Web: www.bookleafpub.com

E-mail: info@bookleafpub.com

ISBN:9789358317077

First edition 2023

Love is Like a Prism

Love is like a prism
both giving and receiving
love refracting and reflecting
in raindrops against the glass
of our shared love

The more dimensions
in our beautiful prism,
the greater the distribution
of bright light and joy
of our shared love

Your love is eternal
both receiving and giving
reflecting all the beauty
in brilliant rainbows
of our shared love

Flannery O'Conner and Me

"I write because I don't know what I think
until I read what I say." ~ Flannery O'Connor~

Nearly every day I stop and consider why I
take on the struggle and challenge to write.
I think I wade deep into my poetry because
I can be myself with language and words. I
love the tumble and sound of words that don't
ever leave me. Deep in my soul I know
what I'm trying to clearly say or what
I'm hoping to discover and share, but I
recognize this requires me to think
about words with pencil scratches until
rhythms and rhymes emerge. It is then I
really understand what I say and read.
I often smile when my scribbles reveal what
has been somersaulting in my brain. Then I
can finally share what I really wanted to say.

*A Golden Shovel

Shifting Paradigms

He cut me off in traffic
and I wanted to rage
but I caught myself
as he swerved toward the
hospital emergency entrance
with panic on his face and
clinched hands gripping
the steering wheel
My rage turned to prayer
for a stranger who
cut me off in traffic

A Siren Call to Education

She was meant to be a teacher
She had chalk dust in her veins
Perhaps it was fate or destiny
Deep down, she was a teacher

She considered her options
She explored industry and business
Opened herself to new opportunities
She was meant to be a teacher

She was a lover of history and books
Always reading and writing on the side
She never recoiled from the siren call
She had chalk dust in her veins

It may have been by chance
Or an unsolicited challenge
Some might say she was called
Perhaps it was fate or destiny

No matter the critical driving forces
Reconciling many painful realities
She surrendered to what she knew
Deep down, she was a teacher

Pink Carnations

This is just routine, you told me
a follow-up and nothing more, but you
invited me to come with you anyway.

You graciously asked me to carry
bunches of pink carnations and
you brought spicy Chana Masala.

This seemed odd but you have always
been your own kind of person and
I never questioned your eccentricities.

We sat quietly as Dr. Smith reviewed the lab
report you brought to him from the oncologist.
You positioned yourself to avoid looking at me.

His solemn eyes and ashen face said it all,
but you were resolute and continued to
look only at him with tear-brimmed eyes

One question he asked quietly. "How long?"
"Just long enough to say my good-byes,"
and with that your discussion ended.

You handed him the warm Chana Masala
"I know it's your favorite and I wanted
to share it with you and express my thanks."

It was then you finally looked at me
no words ~ only eyes filled with love
and then you handed him a pink carnation.

Each person we saw thereafter received
a beautiful pink carnation and a smile
You were living your truth with dignity.

*Oct. 13th is Breast Cancer Awareness Day

It's Starting to Feel Like Spring

The whispers of springtime
are so gentle and sweet
like caresses on my face

The dogs walk a little slower
as they linger and sniff the
the tender flowers just emerging

We gaze heavenward and watch
as a gaggle of geese prepare to fly
knowing their southern respite is over

Soon we will hear the chicklets
join lovely songbirds in a melody strong
as life renews with each tiny hatchling

Other critters frolic with joy anew
as squirrels scramble from tree to tree
encouraging bunnies to peek and play

Springtime always offers sweet promises
of renewal and hope and opportunity
in the bright and beautiful days ahead.

I Need to Read!

Don't interrupt me as read
Of gallant knights on valiant steads
Or children planting magic seeds.
I need to read! I need to read!

Of times and places here and past
My heroes rising from the ash
I crave these tales from vaults amassed
These stories last! These stories last!

I gently sit with books in hand.
To slip away just as I've planned.
To wild quests in distant lands.
It's my dreamland. It's my dreamland.

To read, to dream, to think, to know
It's always been my place to go.
Stories and books help me to grow.
And now you know! And now you know.

Don't interrupt me as read
Words are the food on which I feed
With books in stacks, I'm pleased indeed.
I love to read! I love to read!

What is Normal?

I beg, what is normal?
Heated caustic radical debates
proving normal does not exist
not in a way that is familiar
or even desirable

My normal is gone
like a lost toy or torn book
or like grandma's locket
it's never coming back
just like grandma

I am acutely aware
of the stages of grief
omnipresent in society
not an orderly progression
but in a messy pile of emotions

There is no cycle or pyramid
no timeline to plan or prepare
just anger and bargaining
steeped in vacuous depression
laced with gaseous denial

How I ache for a day when acceptance
becomes normal for long stretches
and hearts are softened toward others
and we enfold and embrace gently
just like grandma

Love Whisperer

In my dream, I was surrounded
by astounding and wonderful people
being lauded and praised
for talents and gifts immeasurable

I pulled back to watch in amazement
artists, writers, scientists, and doctors
public speakers and philosophers
changing the world in purposeful ways

I wondered to myself: what is my gift?
and then I was pulled into an embrace
My beautiful child, a spirit whispered
Don't you know? You're a whisperer.

I don't understand what that means.
You are a love whisperer to all
Animals and children feel it first
You radiate love in all you do

Remember, you collect hugs and tears
You listen to stories and hold hands
Strangers are drawn to your heart
You are, my sweetest, a love whisperer

And then I awoke and smiled to myself
Was this just a silly dream? Do I have a gift?
Yes, my darling, said the spirit once again
Being a love whisperer is a gift that matters
most.

Mirror, Mirror on the Wall ~ When Chemo Has Its Way!

"Mirror, mirror on the wall.
Who's the fairest one of all?"
"Why ask me, my dear sweet child?
Is this ride called life, both frightful and wild?

Are you feeling sad about falling locks?
I see it's time we have one of our talks.
My dearest darling, it's not the hair
That makes you beautiful and fair.

Look deeper in your soul and heart
For that's where Beauty has her start.
Now take a look at your eyes so bright,
And smile and laugh with great delight.

For appearance is fickle thing,
Let it go, open up and sing."
"Thank you, Mirror on the wall
This sage advice on my ears do fall.

Today, instead of bemoaning loss,
I'll walk and laugh, all cares to toss.
My hair may fall, and I'll let it go.
And in good time, it will once again grow.

"Mirror, mirror on the wall.
I am the fairest one of all!"
For beauty isn't on the surface, I see.
It's deep inside both you and me."

Feminist is not an F-Word!

I'm fed up with the feeling
that being called a feminist
is an insult – a flagrant
brazen condemnation
of women who are fighting
to be given opportunities to
follow their dreams,
fulfill their aspirations and
find joy in their lives

Stop and think! If
your mother, sister, wife
or friend should have
the same opportunities
you enjoy, shouldn't
you call yourself a
feminist too?
Quit cursing at me!
Feminist is not an F-Word!

Imagine a World

just imagine a world
of all green lights
even for one day
a never-before day

where the work commute
is reduced by half
because every stop light
doesn't ever stop us

and air pollution is
also reduced by half
because no car is
idling and puffing exhaust

and nobody is screaming
for the blasted light
to change and we
just smile and wave

arriving at our destination
happy and ready for
a wonderful and relaxed
start to our workday

wouldn't it be great
even for one day
to imagine a world
of all green lights

When Art Meets the Real World

artful brush strokes
rolling and undulating
against the evening sky
smoothed and dappled
as if the real world is
upside down and inside out
viewing waves from the
depths of the ocean much
like cherished paintings and
the incredible craftsmanship
of Vincent Van Gogh

and yet harsh painted lines
rough pavements and
grating grinding engines
roughly tear us back
to an unforgiving reality
of man against nature
ripping and destroying the
very fabric of our existence
and forsaking nature's
perfect artistry

The Taste of Words

Have you ever considered
that words have a taste
notice that crunch and crisp
are salty and sharp

There are words like
pungent and piquant
that are bitter and biting
and are even harder to say

I hate the feel of words
like acerbic and acrid
that are sour and spiteful
almost acidic in my mouth

I also appreciate words
like charm and choice
that are simple and savory
Comfortable easy words

The best words of all are
words like tender and touch
that are sweet and soothing
gentle words that taste like love.

What Is Heaven?

Is it a quiet soft pastel sunrise
        or the tiny pink and white buds
        on the gnarly old apple tree?

Is heaven the old front porch
        where you shared a first kiss
        with the love of your heart?

Maybe heaven is a slow walk
        with an aging dog who has been
        your faithful companion for years?

It might be that heaven is a cup'a chili
        and a Frosty from Wendy's
        with some dear old friends.

Heaven might be in the fishing boat
        with Grandpa who can tie lures
        faster than you can tie your shoes.

I think heaven is felt in the hugs
        and smiles and tears shared with
        friends at weddings and funerals.

Perhaps heaven isn't a place
      but instead, it is whatever genuinely
      fills your heart and makes you happy.

So, why do we wait to die to enjoy Heaven?
      Perhaps it's all around us and we
      Just need to slow down and enjoy it.

Wisdom in the Trees

I find deep wisdom in the trees
a strong sense of comradery
a humble bond of unity

it seems they grow with simple ease
straight and stately through sun and storm
a godly grace – majestic form

I oft neglect both roots and knees
the hidden force of endurance
a woodland strengthened in purpose

Distracted by the gentle breeze
I must look to my foundation
nurture seeds of my formation.

I too have roots much like the trees
to support sustain and flourish
those deep roots connect and nourish

and this is guidance I must seize
eternal truths by which I live
each day to breathe and share and give

Sharing Seeds

The story was once told of an old farmer
who shared the best of his seed corn
with all the farmers in his town.

"Are these not the very people
with whom you compete at
the county fair?" chided his friend.

"That is exactly why I share,"
said the old farmer with a wise
look and a warm and tender smile.

"Inferior corn from other plants will
cross-pollinate my fields. In the end,
none of the corn is any good."

So it is with life. When we share
the best of ourselves with others,
we are all better for it.

Button, Button ~ Who's Got the Button?

Tucked into the sewing cupboard
is a tidy little box containing
buttons collected over the years
Tiny buttons of all varieties
matched and unmatched
gathered from old clothes
and stitched into new clothes
to replace the button that
was lost and never found.

In my collection are tiny buttons that
once adorned handmade clothes
sewn for my babies who are grown
There are buttons clipped from
old shirts and saved just in case
There are old wooden buttons
and some crafted from shells
Some mass-produced for uniforms
and others unique and playful.

I recall my momma's button box
I would spend hours sorting and
playing with the buttons
sometimes creating stories to

fuel my wild imagination
with buttons that once belonged
to regal queens and majestic kings
or playing a game with my sibs
"Button, button -- who's got the button?"

Now and then I wonder what
happened to my momma's box?
I look at my own collection that
bears no memory for anyone but me
Perhaps that's why I write poems
about things like buttons and games
to preserve in this fleeting moment
the memories that slip away like
buttons that are lost forever.

Keep on Keepin' On!

The hum of electronics is silent
and the sound of songbirds and frogs
changes the ambiance of evening.

The power's out and I sit on the front porch
like an old relic from generations past –
rocking gently in the old chair

I hold a small crochet hook in my hand
and work carefully on a hand-made project
Loop over the hook pull through and repeat

I think I'm not so different from Grandma
with her arthritic gnarled knuckles
and slowly numbing fingers.

She was hardworking and industrious
I remember her pragmatic advice:
"Just keep on keepin' on, sweet girl."

I wonder sometimes if the perception
of simpler times is wishful thinking –
a hope rather than a reality.

Perhaps it wasn't simpler but rather
more focused on self-sufficiency
and making do with what they had.

So I stretch and shake my hands carefully,
I smile and appreciate that Grandma's lessons
and her sweet love of life lives on in me.

I pick up the hook and loop the yarn over
my fingers and hum along to an old song
'cuz there's "peace in the valley for me."

Why I Write Poetry

I love words
because they leave a trail
memories and reflections.

Poems and prose
like snapshots in the moment
pause and breathe

Glimmers of hope
the rhythms of daily life
insights and musings

Sharing my thoughts
in words I feel deeply
gentle heart murmurs

Expressions of hope
sharing with those I love
laughter and encouragement

I love words
the essence of who I am
moments of joy

Letting Go

I've discovered something about myself
I am not having a crisis of faith,
but rather a crisis of traditions.
I see that as my world enlarges
many of the things I was led to believe
are just long-held cultural practices.
I'm ready to push against archaic
traditions and readily embrace change.

One truth I hold near and dear to my heart
is that I'm a beloved, precious daughter
of heavenly parents ~ my creators
who have trusted me to reflect their love
to all children without judgment or malice.
When the long day comes that I am embraced
in the arms of my mother and father,
I'll rest in the peace of their eternal love.